T0113685

FANNIE MAE'S

COUNTRY SOUL FOOD COOKBOOK

FANNIE D EVANS

authorHOUSE

AuthorHouse™
1663 Liberty Drive
Bloomington, IN 47403
www.authorhouse.com
Phone: 833-262-8899

Published by AuthorHouse 09/02/2022

ISBN: 978-1-6655-7029-9 (sc)
ISBN: 978-1-6655-7028-2 (e)

Print information available on the last page.

Any people depicted in stock imagery provided by Getty Images are models, and such images are being used for illustrative purposes only. Certain stock imagery © Getty Images.

This book is printed on acid-free paper.

Because of the dynamic nature of the Internet, any web addresses or links contained in this book may have changed since publication and may no longer be valid. The views expressed in this work are solely those of the author and do not necessarily reflect the views of the publisher, and the publisher hereby disclaims any responsibility for them.

CONTENTS

INTRODUCTION

I was born and raised in Lawrence, MS. I am the daughter of Authur and Rosie Lee Dukes. My entire life revolves around southern cooking and southern living. For breakfast, we would have homemade biscuits with eat-well salmon. Sometimes, we would have biscuits and tomato gravy, biscuits, sugar syrup, or with fat back meat.

We had a vegetable garden. My mother and father would call it the "truck patch". I can remember when my father was a sharecropper.

We were living in a little shack. Early in the morning, the dew would fall on our faces, because we had a leak on our tin roof. We also had a tin heater. We would all gather around that one heater to try to stay warm. We cooked on a wood stove, but this was long before microwaves. My momma used to make soap with red devil lye and harmony in a big black wash pot.

When I was a teenager, I started staying with my aunt and uncle. I would go into the kitchen and watch my aunt cook. She would teach me different things about cooking. I will never forget she told me "Cooking is something that you have to love because it shows through the dishes you've prepared."

I must give my husband credit, Minister Larry Evans, He would not let me quit nor give up. He is always pushing me to keep on writing recipes. This is partly the reason I was able to compose this cookbook. Also, I truly thank God for He is the Man who made it all possible for me.

CAKES

PEACH POUND CAKE

2 sticks of unsalted butter (soften)
2 c. of sugar
4 eggs
1 tsp. of peach flavoring
1 tsp. of baking powder
1 tsp. of salt
2 ¾ c. of all-purpose flour
2 c. of cubed peaches

Preheat oven to 325 degrees. Grease a tube baking pan with butter and flour then set aside. Beat butter and sugar then add eggs to mixture (one at a time). Mix in peach flavoring. In a separate bowl mix baking powder, salt, and 2 2/4 cup of flour (sifted). With mixer running on low speed, add flour mixture to butter mixture beat until combined.

Combine peaches and remaining ¼ cup of flour in a bowl. Toss flour and peaches until the peaches are coated. Fold peaches into cake batter and spread evenly in the tube pan. Bake for 1 hour and 10 minutes

PEACH GLAZE

1 tbsp. Cornstarch
1 cup of peaches (smashed)
¼ cup of sugar
¼ cup of water

Stir together ¼ cup of water to 1 tbsp. of corn starch then add 1 cup of smash peaches and sugar in a saucepan. Bring to a boil. Drizzle over pound cake.

BANANA POUND CAKE

1 box of pound cake mix
2 c. self-rising flour
½ c. sugar
1 ¾ c. milk
4 eggs
2 sticks of melted butter
1 c. mashed banana
½ c. chopped nuts

Preheat oven to 325 degrees. Mix 1 box of cake mix with 2 cups of self-rising flour, add sugar, milk, eggs, butter, and mashed bananas. Fold in nuts. Bake for 1 hour and 15 minutes.

BOX POUND CAKE

1 box pound cake mix
2 c. self-rising flour
2c. sugar
1 ¾ c. milk
4 eggs
2 sticks of melted butter
1 ½ tsp. vanilla flavoring
1 ½ tsp. coconut flavoring
1 ½ tsp. almond flavoring

Mix 1 box pound cake mix, flour, and sugar together. Add milk eggs, butter, and flavorings. Bake at 325 degrees for one hour and 15 minutes

Icing
Use 1 16 oz. Cream Cheese Icing, add 1 cup of chopped pecans to cream cheese icing. Mix well then put the Icing on your cake. Be sure to let it cool before icing.

APPLE CAKE

2. c Sugar
2 large eggs
1 ½ c vegetable oil
2 ½ c. self-rising flour
1 ½ tbsp. cinnamon
2 tsp. vanilla extract
3 c. chopped raw apples
1 c. chopped nuts mixed with a little flour

Beat oil and sugar together, add eggs then flour. Add cinnamon and vanilla to mixture. Beat until smooth. Mix in nuts and apples. Pour in a greased (floured) tube pan. Bake at 325 degrees for 55-60 minutes. Let it cool before removing from the pan.

Icing
½ c. brown sugar
1 small can of Pet evaporated milk
1 tsp. vanilla flavoring
¼ c. chopped pecans
Stir until thick overheat.

BUMPS AND LUMP CAKE

Stir with a large spoon only!!!

2 c/ sugar
1 ¼ c. vegetable oil
4 eggs
3 c. Swan cake flour
2 ½ tsp. baking powder
1 ½ c. milk
6 tsp lemon flavoring
1 c. pineapple chunks (cut into smaller pieces)
½ c. pecans (broken or chopped)
½ c. raisins
½ c maraschino cherries

Combine the flour with baking powder and put to the side. Stir sugar and oil together, add eggs then flour and baking powder combination and stir. Add milk, lemon flavoring, pineapples, pecans, raisins, cherries and stir. Bake in a 3 qt. Pyrex dish. Bake at 350 degrees for 50 minutes.

Use Cream cheese or lemon frosting.

CHOCOLATE CHIP BUNDT CAKE

1 box devil's food cake mix (Duncan Hines)
4 large eggs
1 small box of vanilla instant pudding mix
¾ c. vegetable oil
1c/ chocolate chips
½ c. frozen strawberries
½ c. water
1 ¼ confectioners' sugar.

Preheat oven to 350 degrees. Mix cake mix, eggs, ½ c. water, pudding, and oil in a large bowl. Beat with an electric mixer. Fold in chocolate chips. Pour mixture into a greased (floured) Bundt cake pan. Bake for 1 hour.

Glaze
Combine ½ c. frozen strawberries (drained) mix with 1 ¼ c. confectioners' sugar. Drizzle glaze on cake.

STRAWBERRY CAKE

1 box yellow cake mix (Duncan Hines)
1 c. self-rising flour
4 eggs
1 c. vegetable oil
1 small box of strawberry Jell-o
½ c. sugar
1 16 oz. frozen strawberries

Stir together cake mix, flour, eggs, oil, sugar, and Jell-O. Add ½ box of the frozen strawberries (with juice from the strawberries) to cake mix. Bake in 9-inch baking dish at 325 degrees for 1 hour.

Icing
Drain the remaining frozen strawberries.
½ stick of butter
2 c. confectioners' sugar
4 oz. cream cheese
Drop of red food coloring

Mix all ingredients and spread on top of cake.

COCONUT PINEAPPLE CAKE

1 box yellow cake mix (Duncan Hines)
1 c. flour
4 eggs
1 c. vegetable oil
1 large can of crushed pineapples
1 small bag of flaked coconut

Stir together cake mix, eggs, oil, and flour. Add ½ c. crush pineapple (including juice) to cake mix. Bake in a 9 in. baking dish at 325 degrees for 1 hour.

Icing
½ stick butter
1 c. sugar
2tbsp. flour
The remaining crushed pineapples

Combine ingredients and cook in a small boiler until thicken. Spread over cake then sprinkle with coconut.

BLUEBERRY MUFFINS

1 – 7 oz. package blueberry muffin mix
¼ c. self-rising flour
½ c. milk
1 egg
2 tbsp. of vegetable oil

Grease muffins pan with oil. Sprinkle the bottom with flour. Mix all ingredients in a medium size bowl. Makes six muffins. Bake at 400 degrees for 15 minutes.

STRAWBERRY MUFFINS

1 – 7 oz. package strawberry muffin mix
¼ c. self-rising flour
½ c. milk
1 egg
2 tbsp of vegetable oil

Grease muffins pan with oil. Sprinkle the bottom with flour. Mix all ingredients in a medium size bowl. Bake at 400 degrees for 15 minutes. Makes six muffins

PIES

STRAWBERRY PUDDING

2 c. carnation milk
1 box cook & serve vanilla pudding
1 tbsp of strawberry gelatin
½ c. frozen sliced sugar strawberries
1-10oz. bag vanilla wafers
1 medium size whipped topping

In a medium size saucepan stir 2 cups of milk and pudding mix. Add strawberry gelatin, frozen strawberries, bring to a boil over medium heat. Stir constantly.

In a dish layer vanilla wafers and pudding. Top with whipped topping.

MUSCADINE JELLY

6 c. muscadines
1 box Sure Jell
5 c. muscadine juice
7 c. sugar
½ tsp. lemon juice

Boil muscadines for 30 minutes. Drain them. Cook in large boiler. Stir in sure jell and lemon juice. Bring to a rolling boil (stir constantly). Stir in sugar and let it come to a rolling boil again. Remove from heat and skin of foam.

APPLE COBBLER

1 stick of butter
1 c. sugar
1 c. self-rising flour
2/3 cup of milk
Dash of cinnamon
1 tsp. vanilla
1 large can of sliced apples

Melt butter in a baking dish. Mix flour, sugar, milk, vanilla, and cinnamon well. Pour batter in baking dish over the melted butter. Do NOT stir. Put apples and juice on top. Bake at 400 degrees for 40 minutes.

PEACH COBBLER

1 stick butter
1 c. sugar
1 c. self-rising flour
2/3 c. milk
Dash of cinnamon
1 tsp. vanilla
1 large can of sliced peaches

Melt butter in a baking dish. Mix flour, sugar, milk, vanilla, and cinnamon well. Pour batter in baking dish over the melted butter. Do NOT stir. Put peaches and juice on top. Bake at 400 degrees for 40 minutes.

CANDIED YAMS

5 medium size sweet potatoes
2 c. water
1 c. sugar
2 tsp. vanilla flavoring
½ tsp. cinnamon
2 tbsp. margarine

Peel and cut sweet potatoes. Cook sweet potatoes, water, and sugar over medium heat. When sweet potatoes are tender, add vanilla flavoring, cinnamon, and margarine.

BUTTERMILK PIE

2- ¼ c. sugar
1-1/4 stick butter
4 eggs
3 tbsp flour
1 c. buttermilk
2 tsp. vanilla flavoring
1 tsp. coconut flavoring
2 uncooked pie shells

Preheat oven to 400 degrees. Cream sugar, butter, eggs, and flour together. Add buttermilk, vanilla, and coconut flavoring. Stir for a few minutes. Pour in each pie shell. Bake for 50 minutes.

PECAN PIE

3 eggs
1 c. karo light or dark syrup
1 c. sugar
2 tbsp. margarine (melted)
1 ¼ tsp. vanilla flavoring
1 ½ c. pecans
1 unbaked 9 in. pie crust

Mix all five ingredients together except for pecans. Stir in pecans. Bake at 350 degrees for 50-55 minutes. Be sure to preheat oven if pie crust is frozen.

DIABETIC LEMON PIE

1 c. water
1 c. real lemon juice
1 c. sugar
2 tbsp. corn starch
1 tsp. lemon flavoring
Yellow food coloring (few drops)
1 graham cracker crust
Whip cream

Combine all ingredients and cook on low heat until ready. Pour into pie crust. Let cool and put whip cream on top.

OLD FASHIONED LEMON PIE

3 eggs yolks
1 can condensed milk
½ c. real lemon juice
½ tsp. cream of tartar
1 graham cracker crust

Pie filling
Mix eggs, condensed milk, and lemon juice together and set aside.

Meringue
3 egg whites
1/3 c. sugar
½ tsp. cream of tartar

Beat the egg whites until fluffy. Add sugar and cream of tartar. Pour the filling into pie crust. Topped with meringue. Bake at 325 degrees until the meringue is browned.

RAISIN PIE

3 eggs
1 c. sugar
½ tsp. cinnamon
½ tsp. nutmeg
¼ tsp. salt
2 ½ tbsp. real lemon juice
2 tbsp. butter (melted)
1 ¼ c. raisins
½ c. walnuts or pecans (chopped)
1- 8 in. unbaked pastry shell

Combine all 7 ingredients (except for the raisins and nuts). Mix well. Stir in raisins and nuts. Pour into pastry pie shell. Bake at 375 degrees for 40 minutes or until the filling is set.

SWEET POTATO PIE

2 c. sugar
1 stick oleo
3 eggs
Dash of nutmeg
2 c. smashed sweet potatoes
1 can small pet milk
2 tbsp. flour
1 tbsp. vanilla flavoring
2 unbaked frozen pie shells

Cream sugar, oleo, and eggs (1 egg at a time). Add sweet potatoes, flour, milk, cinnamon, and vanilla flavoring. Pour in unbaked pie shells. Bake at 350 degrees for 45 minutes.

MEATS

FRIED CHICKEN

1 c. self-rising
1 tbsp. seasoned Salt
1 cut up chicken
½ c. whole milk
Vegetable oil

Combine flour and seasoned salt. Dip each piece of chicken in milk (one piece at a time) then coat with flour mixture. Be sure to coat each piece well. Heat oil in a skillet. Add chicken to hot oil and cook until browned on all sides. Turn often. Cook on medium heat. Drain cooked pieces on paper towel.

HAMBURGER STEAK

2 ½ lbs. ground beef
2 eggs
1 tbsp. seasoned salt
1 ½ tbsp self-rising flour
1 tbsp. minced onion or real onion

Mix all ingredients. Roll the patties into a large size. Place patties in a large skillet with lid. Cook on low heat until browned on both sides. Drain fat. Serve with brown gravy and onions.

SALMON CROQUETTES

2 cans of pink salmon
1 large, chopped onion
4 large eggs
1 tbsp. Of seasoned salt
2 tbsp. Of flour
2 tbsp. Of corn meal
1 c. vegetable oil

Clean all bones from the salmon. Mash the salmon with a large spoon in a bowl then add all ingredients. Heat vegetable oil in a medium sized skillet. Use a large spoon to drop them in the grease. Brown on both sides.

SOUTHERN STYLE SMOTHERED PORK CHOPS

1 ½ c. vegetable oil
5 pork chops
1 tbsp. seasoned salt
2 c. self-rising flour
1 tbsp minced onion or real onion
2 tbsp chopped bell pepper
2 ½ c. water

Heat oil in a skillet. Sprinkle seasoned salt on the pork chops, flour it, and fry. Once meat is fried place into a Pyrex 3 qt. dish. Sprinkle onion and bell pepper over the meat then add water. Cover with foil. Bake at 400 degrees for 40-45 minutes.

BAKED CHICKEN

1 cut up chicken

1 tbsp. Seasoned salt

1 tbsp. Rotisserie seasoning

1 tbsp. Minced onion or real onion

1 tsp. Garlic powder

1 tsp. Montreal chicken seasoning

Mix all ingredients. Be sure to coat the chicken well. Place in a 3-quart Pyrex dish. Then cover with foil. Let it marinate for 30 minutes. Bake in the oven at 400 degrees for 40 minutes. Take the foil off and place back in the oven for 5 more minutes. Cover with foil until served.

CHICKEN AND DUMPLINGS

1 10.5oz. Can of cream of chicken
1 ½ 10.5 oz. Can of water
1/8 tsp. Black pepper
2 tbsp. Butter or vegetable oil spread
1/8 salt
1 ½ c. self-rising flour
1/3 c. cold water
1 ½ c chopped chicken

Combine cream of chicken, water, black pepper, butter, and salt together. Bring to a boil on low heat then add chopped chicken.

Make dumplings with flour and cold water (from refrigerator). Roll them out. Cut them into squares. Drop them into chopped chicken mixture. Cook on low heat for 10 minutes.

PACIFIC WHITING FISH

Whiting fish (thawed)
1 c. self-rising flour
1 c. self-rising cornmeal
1/8 tsp. black pepper
Seasoned salt of choice
2 ½ c. vegetable oil

Mix cornmeal and flour in a gallon bag. Sprinkle salt and pepper on your fillets. Dredge each piece in your corn meal and flour mixture. Fry fillets in hot oil until browned. Drain on paper towel.

FRIED CATFISH FILLETS

Catfish fillets (thawed)
1 c. self-rising flour
1 c. self-rising corn meal
1/8 tsp. black pepper
Seasoned salt of choice
2 ½ c. vegetable oil

Mix, corn meal, and flour in a gallon bag. Sprinkle salt and pepper on your fillets. Dredge each piece in your cornmeal and flour mixture. Fry fillets in hot oil until browned. Drain on paper towel.

PORK LOIN

5 slices pork loin
½ c. oil
1 pkg. brown gravy
1 tbsp. flour
2 c. water
2 tsp. seasoned salt
1 tbsp. minced onion

Season pork loin with salt. Fry them in oil. Mix 1 pkg. of brown gravy and flour together, add water, and onions to meat. Cook on low heat for 15 minutes.

BEEF MEATLOAF

1 ½ lb. ground beef
2 eggs (beaten)
½ medium bell pepper (chopped)
½ c. ketchup
2 tbsp. flour
1 ½ tbsp. minced onion
½ tsp. seasoned salt

Mix beef, eggs, bell pepper, ketchup, flour, onion, and seasoned salt. Cook at 375 degrees in oven. Drain the meat. Topped with ¾ c. ketchup.

SLOPPY JOE

1-15oz. can of Manwich original
1-14.5 oz. can of diced tomatoes
2 tbsp. chopped onions
2 tsp. sugar
1 small package ground beef.

In a medium skillet brown ground beef and drain. Mix the remaining ingredients together. Cook for 15 minutes.

GREENS, VEGETABLES AND BEANS

FRIED SWEET POTATOES

3 medium sweet potatoes
½ stick of butter
1/3 c. sugar
¼ c. water
1/8 tsp. Cinnamon
1/8 tsp. vanilla flavoring

Peel, slice, and wash sweet potatoes. Fry slices in butter over medium heat. Use a skillet with lid. Let both sides brown. Then add sugar, water, cinnamon, and vanilla. Place the lid on and let it steam until sugar melts.

EGGS AND WILD ONIONS

2c. chopped wild onions
3 c. water
2 slices bacon
1 tsp. Salt
½ tsp. Salt
½ tsp. Black pepper
5 eggs

Boil onion for 40 minutes. Drain water from onions. Fry bacon and break into small pieces. Add onions, salt, and pepper. Stir well. Whip five eggs and pour over onions. Stir until done.

PURPLE HULL PEAS

7 c. water
1 large smoked neckbone
6 c. peas
½ tsp. Seasoned salt
1 tsp. Table salt
1 ½ tbsp. Vegetable oil
1 tbsp. Sugar

Put 7 cups of water and neckbone in a medium sized boiler. Boil for 15 minutes then add the remaining ingredients. Cook for 50 minutes. Add water if necessary.

BABY LIMA BEANS

5 c. water
1 smoked neckbone
4 c. of lima beans
2 tsp. vegetable oil
1/8 tsp black pepper
1 tsp seasoned salt

In a medium sized boiler, boil neckbone in water for 30 minutes. Add beans and remaining ingredients. Boil until beans are tender.

FRESH FRIED OKRA

¾ c. cooking oil
5 c. of cut up okra
½ tsp. Seasoned salt
½ c. self-rising corn meal

Wash okra and let it drain. Cut it up. Season with seasoned salt. Coat it with corn meal. Make sure the oil is hot before placing the okra in the skillet. Fry on medium heat until it is well cooked.

GREEN BEANS WITH IRISH POTATOES

2 ½ c. water
2 medium sized potatoes
1 14.5 oz. can of cut green beans
1/8 tsp. black pepper
½ tsp. seasoned salt
2 tbsp. vegetable oil spread or butter
1/8 tsp. salt
1 tbsp. self-rising flour

In a medium sized boiler, put water, and potatoes. Let it cook for 10 minutes. Add green beans, pepper, seasoned salt, vegetable oil spread, and salt. Mix 1 tablespoon of flour with ¼ c. of water then pour in beans and potatoes mixture. Cook for 5 more minutes.

IRISH POTATO LOGS

2 Large potatoes
¼ tsp. Seasoned salt
¼ c. self-rising flour
¾ c. cooking oil

Peel, cut, and wash potatoes. Cut them into ¼ slices. Put seasoned salt on them. Coat them with flour. Fry them in cooking oil for 15 minutes or until browned on low heat

SOUTHERN STYLE SQUASH

¼ c. oil
3 c. mashed squash
1 tsp. Seasoned salt
1/8 tsp. Black pepper
1 ½ tsp minced onion or real onion
1 tbsp. Self-rising flour
¼ c. water

Mix oil, squash, seasoned salt, pepper, and onions together in a skillet. Cook for 15 minutes. Stir in flour and ¼ c. water. Cook for 5 more minutes.

SWEET SLICED BEETS

1-15oz. can of beets
2 tbsp. apple cider vinegar
2 tbsp. sugar

Combine all three ingredients together. Cook for 15 minutes.

CABBAGE GREENS

1 slice of bacon
½ small cabbage
1 c. water
½ tsp. salt
1/8 tsp. black pepper

Fry bacon in a small boiler. Cut and wash cabbage. Add cabbage, water, salt, and pepper to boiler with bacon. Cook for 12-15 minutes.

TURNIP GREENS

2 c. water
2 tbsp. sugar
2 slices smoke hog jowls or fat back
¼ c. oil
1 tsp. seasoned salt
3 turnip roots (sliced)

Fry meat in a medium boiler. Add your turnip greens, roots, water, sugar, oil, and seasoned salt.

FROZEN SWEET PEAS

1 slice of bacon
1- 12 oz. bag of sweet peas
2 c. water
1 tsp. seasoned salt
1 tsp. sugar

Fry bacon in a medium boiler. Add your peas, water, sugar, and seasoned salt.

GREEN BEANS

2 slices of bacon
2-14.5oz cans of cut green beans
2 tbsp. apple cider vinegar
2 tbsp. sugar
1 tsp. minced onions

Drain 1 can of green beans and leave water in the other can. Fry bacon in a saucepan. Dump both cans of green beans in saucepan with bacon. Add vinegar, sugar, minced onion, and salt if needed. Cook for 12 minutes.

BOIL CORN ON THE COB

4 c. water
2 tbsp. margarine
Seasoned salt of choice

Bring water to a boil. Drop corn into boiling water. Boil for 30 minutes.
Drain water off corn. Rub margarine on corn. Sprinkle with seasoned salt.

CORN

1- 15.25 oz. whole kernel corn
1- 15.25 oz. creamed corn
¼ tsp. black pepper
2 tbsp. oleo
1 tbsp. self-rising flour
2 slices of bacon

Drain water off the whole kernel corn and combine with creamed corn then bring to a boil. Mix pepper, oleo, and flour together then cook until thick. Lay your two slices of bacon on top of corn. Drizzle just a little bit of oil on top.

BREADS

BUTTERMILK CORNBREAD

1 c. self-rising cornmeal
2/3 c. self-rising flour
¼ c. oil
1 egg
1 tbsp. sugar
¾ c. buttermilk

Mix cornmeal and flour together. Add oil, egg, sugar, and milk. Pour into a medium size greased cast iron skillet. Be sure to sprinkle cornmeal on the bottom of the skillet. Bake at 400 degrees.

HOMEMADE CORNBREAD

1 c. self-rising cornmeal
2/3 c. self-rising flour
¼ c. oil
1 egg
1 tbsp. sugar
¾ c. whole milk

Mix cornmeal and flour together. Add oil, egg, sugar, and milk. Pour into a medium size greased cast iron skillet. Be sure to sprinkle cornmeal on the bottom of the skillet. Bake at 400 degrees.

CORNMEAL FLAP JACKS

¾ c. self-rising cornmeal
1/2 c. self-rising flour
2 tbsp. oil
1 egg
2 tbsp. sugar
½ c. whole milk

Mix cornmeal and flour together. Add oil, egg, sugar, and milk. Mix well. Use a non-stick skillet with a lid. Put a little cooking oil in the skillet and cook on low heat. Use 2 tbsp. of flap jacks' mixture per flap jack. When browned flip over.

DIABETIC TOAST

2 slices of bread
2 tsp. of margarine
2 tbsp. of apple sauce

Spread margarin on your bread and toast it. Once toasted, spread apple sauce on toast.

CASSEROLES AND POT PIES

CHICKEN PIE

2-15 oz. can of mixed vegetables
2-10.5 oz. can of cream of chicken
1/8 tsp. black pepper
2 chopped boiled eggs
1 ½ c. chopped boiled chicken

Top Crust
1 c. self-rising flour
¼ c. oil
1/3 c. cold water

Filling
Drain water off canned vegetables then mix all 6 ingredients together. Pour into an 8x11 dish.

Crust
Mix flour, oil, and cold water. Roll flour dough with a rolling pin. Lay the crust on top of the filling. Melt ¼ c. margarine then pour on top of chicken pot pie. Bake at 400 degrees until browned.

MACARONI AND CHEESE

4 ½ c. water
1 tbsp. oil
1 ¼ tsp salt
2 ¼ c. elbow macaroni
¼ c. flour
2 tbsp. butter
¼ tsp. black pepper
2 ½ tbsp. margarine
2 c. medium cheddar cheese
1 c. sharp cheddar cheese

Bring water, salt, and oil to a boil. Add macaroni then cook until tender. Stir flour, ¾ c. water, and butter in a bowl. Cook in microwave oven until it thickens then add to drained macaroni. Combine pepper, margarine, and cheese together into the dish. Sprinkle ½ c. sharp cheddar on top and let it melt.

BUTTERED RICE

2 ¼ c. water
1 c. rice
1 tsp. salt
1 tbsp. margarine

In a medium size boiler add water and let it come to a boil. Add rice, salt, and margarine then cook on low heat with lid for 15 minutes. Let it set for 5 minutes before removing the lid.

SQUASH WITH BACON AND CHEESE

3 c. mashed squash
¼ c. oil
1 tsp. Seasoned salt
1/8 tsp black pepper
1 ½ tsp minced onion or real onion
1 tbsp. Self-rising flour
¼ c. water
3 slices bacon
1 8 oz. Shredded sharp cheddar cheese

Mix squash, oil, seasoned salt, pepper, and onion together in a skillet. Cook for 15 minutes. Stir flour and water. Pour over squash. Cook for 5 additional minutes. Pour squash mixture into a 2-quart Pyrex dish. Break bacon into pieces. Spread over squash mixture then add cheese on top. Bake at 400 degrees until cheese melts.

ABOUT THE AUTHOR

I was born in Lawrence, MS. IN Newton County. I went to Lawrence High School and later attended Pilate High School in Newton, MS.

I am a member of Union Chapel Methodist Church of Lawrence, MS. I am wife to Minister Larry Evans of Lawrence, MS. I am the mother of four children. Three of my children live in MS. One of them is deceased. I am one of nine children (seven girls and two boys).

At age twelve, I remember singing in White Stone Baptist Church Choir. As time went by, I started singing with a quartet group called The White Stone Travels Jr. I use to really enjoyed watching and helping the older generations cook on their wooden stoves. This where I can my love for cooking. I give thanks to God for my up bringing and for all that He has done. For He has led and guided me through even until this day.

Printed in the United States
by Baker & Taylor Publisher Services